All the luck

All the luck

Poems celebrating love, life,
and the enduring human spirit

by Sydney Eddison

Pomperaug Valley Press
Newtown, Connecticut

For information:
Pomperaug Valley Press
65 Echo Valley Road
Newtown, CT 06470

ISBN-10: 1984200194
ISBN-13: 9781984200198

First printing: February 2018
Printed in the United States of America

Editor: Lorraine Anderson
Front cover photo: © 2018 by Kimberly Day Proctor
Back cover photo: © 2018 by Hank Meirowitz
Cover and interior design: Barbara Cottingham

Printed by CreateSpace

Also by Sydney Eddison

A Patchwork Garden: Unexpected Pleasures from a Country Garden (1990)

A Passion for Daylilies: The Flowers and the People (1993)

The Unsung Season: Gardens and Gardeners in Winter (1995)

The Self-Taught Gardener: Lessons from a Country Garden (1997)

The Gardener's Palette: Creating Color in the Garden (2003)

Gardens to Go: Creating and Designing a Container Garden (2005)

Gardening for a Lifetime: How to Garden Wiser as You Grow Older (2010)

Where We Walk: Poems Rooted in the Soil of New England (2015)

Fragments of Time: Poems of Gratitude for Everyday Miracles (2016)

for Peter

Table of Contents

Harvest of Years   67

Acknowledgments   96
About the author   97

❧ Preface ❦

*F*or as long as I can remember, I have had a passion for plants, animals, and the Connecticut countryside. These were the subjects of my first poems, written when I was in elementary school. After a hiatus of seventy-five years, I returned to poetry and to these familiar themes in *Where We Walk: Poems Rooted in the Soil of New England* and *Fragments of Time: Poems of Gratitude for Everyday Miracles.*

While this new collection includes nature poems, many more are about living, dying, and finding answers to a question that has stayed in my mind for more than seventy years. At the end of Thornton Wilder's play *Our Town*, Emily Webb asks, "Do any human beings ever realize life while they live it?—every, every minute?" The play's narrator replies: "No." And after a pause, "Saints and poets, maybe—they do some."

Performing the role of Emily in the school play at the age of seventeen, I internalized this lesson, and I have spent a lifetime trying to live by it. But like all who have tried before me and those seekers who will follow, I have found it almost impossible. That is probably one of the reasons I began to write poems again.

Our Town is not just the story of a quaint New England village full of stock characters—the editor of the local paper; the doctor, who delivers babies and sets broken bones; the sad, bitter town drunk; the minister, who officiates at weddings and funerals, and in this play, serves as the narrator. The power of this play lies in the simple humanity of the characters and the belief that "there's something way down deep that's eternal about every human being." Every poem I write is an attempt to find that *something.*

All the Luck

Yesterday I drove the road
I once traveled daily,
back and forth to work
that I enjoyed, teaching students
of whom I was fond,
and returning home
to my spouse or sometimes
meeting him for dinner
halfway between.
What full years those were!
We both had satisfying jobs
and a house we loved,
full of pets and visitors.
"We've been shot through
with luck," he would say.
And it was true, always,
even at the end.
As I was helping him
to turn over—he was
very ill by this time—
he murmured, "I'll bet you
never thought you'd
be doing this."
My reply was that
I never thought I would
be so lucky.

Now and Then

Boxing Day

On this first day
after Christmas, or Boxing Day
as it was known
in Edwardian England,
it was customary to give
presents to the servants,
a tradition my English mother
remembered from her youth.
I always loved her stories
of growing up in Liverpool
before the First World War.
To an American child,
her life sounded as romantic
and alluring as a fairy tale.
No wonder my mother missed
the world she had traded
for a struggling doctor and
an old schoolhouse
in the Connecticut countryside.

As the Twig Is Bent

Growing up with two brothers
made it obvious to me
that it was better
to be a boy than
a girl. So I did
the next best thing and
set about becoming a tomboy
who could arm wrestle and win
and pitch a baseball—
hard and fast.
While these talents did not
prove valuable in adolescence,
they served me well when
my husband and I bought
an old farmhouse and several
overgrown acres
in need of a gardener.
It was a perfect fit.
We took possession in January;
I began digging in March
and have been at it
ever since, admittedly
with less vigor now,
but no less enthusiasm.

Winter Now and Then

This morning the flowerpots
on the terrace looked like
giant cupcakes with white frosting.
It had snowed all night
and the stuff was still
coming down.
But at noon, the crew
that mows in the summer
came and plowed us out.
Now it is snowing again!
It reminds me of my youth.
This is what winters
were like in those days.
I remember once having to
shovel snow off the roof.
It was exciting to be
up so high doing something
useful and grown up.
I have always liked winter.

Community

In my town, Christmas begins
with the eagerly awaited
Greens Sale, showcasing the talents
of the local garden club.
Members fill the nave
of the old Congregational church
with wreaths, garlands, and
the resinous scent
of balsam fir.
For days, the women have
labored downstairs in the undercroft.
Using fine green wire, they
bind together bunches of holly,
spruce, juniper, and pine, shaping
them into unique decorations
embellished with cones, berries,
and dry seedpods.
Their work is as creative
as it is beautiful.
But it isn't the ornaments
alone that attract so many
to this annual event.
It is the strong sense
of community—women working together,
like quilters of the past.
Everyone participates.
That's why people are waiting
in the cold on the
first Saturday in December.
All belong to this fellowship.

Holiday Memories

Christmas always triggers memories
of childhood, when my father,
game but unconvincing, would
play Santa Claus and call
down the chimney to
my younger brother and me.
"Have you been good children?"
he would ask.
We would assure him
that we had.
Decades later, he spent his
last Christmas in our guestroom
in a hospital bed,
my mother at his side.

Even then, he enjoyed
the holiday and insisted that
I bake shortbread from his
old Fanny Farmer's cookbook.
He inspected each tray as
it came from the oven.
For years after he died,
I baked shortbread every Christmas,
but eventually my enthusiasm flagged.
It has been a long
time now since I've done
any holiday baking,
but maybe this year
I will start again.

Sound and Silence

That year, after the holidays
life began to unravel.
First, a fender bender—
unremarkable except that my husband
was such a good driver.
Inexplicably, he had blacked out
for a second.
Sometime after that,
he developed a persistent,
hacking cough that turned into
pneumonia, from which he recovered,
only to learn that
a new, ominous rattling
sound in his chest
was lung cancer.
Two weeks later,
he was gone, leaving behind
silence in the house
and a gaping hole
in my heart.

Keepsakes

Although the festival of Epiphany
ended more than a week ago,
my Christmas tree still stands.
Today I will finally start
removing the ornaments,
each beloved and many handmade.
From a niece in Scotland,
angels robed in blue
with golden wings.
A little white dog
with a red collar
felted by a friend
of a friend.
And most precious of all,
the origami cranes made
by my husband
the year we were married.
These keepsakes are why my tree
remains standing in mid-January.

Sharing

I hate an unmade bed,
and mine often is nowadays.
I blame the dog,
who shares it—
she's not an early riser.
It's funny, the way couples
decide who sleeps on which
side of a double bed.
From the start, I gravitated
to the left; my spouse,
to the right.
He was tall and fully
occupied his side, while Abby,
our first Jack Russell Terrier,
slept under my feet.
That way, there was
just enough room
for the three of us.

.

A Bargain

A terrier in the house
means that you do not
live alone but share
your life with an entertaining,
sometimes exasperating
companion who barks for service,
expects to be let in
and out on demand, and
insists on an interesting walk
daily and three square meals.
In return, you get
a warm body
in your bed at night
and cheerful company wherever
you go all day long.
I call that a bargain.

Quiet on the Home Front

I wonder what she hears.
You can tell she's listening
by the alert carriage
of her button-down ears.
But for the moment, nothing
interests her enough to rouse
her from the comfort
of my lap.
She heaves a sigh, makes
a one-hundred-and-eighty-
degree turn, and tucks
her head underneath my arm.
On duty, she marks
every falling leaf, and even
in repose, her acute senses
idle while she naps,
ready in an instant should
the need for action arise.
This morning, all is quiet
on the home front, and
she can afford to sleep in.

Cleaning Day

Once a month an efficient
young woman arrives
at my house to clean.
Today she has a helper,
and they converse in Portuguese,
voices raised above the hum
of the vacuum cleaner.
Meanwhile, the dog and I
scuttle from room to room,
keeping just ahead of them.
But they are quick, and
now we are trapped
in my office, waiting for
the kitchen floor to dry.
At last the girls call out
their goodbyes, and we are
free to come downstairs
and admire their handiwork.

Groundhog Day

As folklore would have it,
groundhogs awaken
from their winter dormancy
on the second of February.
They are said to emerge
from their burrows
to observe the weather.
If it is sunny, they
see their own shadows,
take fright, and hurry
back to bed.

While I have never seen
a groundhog before mid-March,
the dog, ever hopeful, pauses
on our daily walks
to stare at an abandoned building,
where one of these stout,
placid rodents spends
its somnolent winters.
Phoebe strains at her leash,
but I tell her, "Not today."
Disappointed, she trots on.

A Tribute to Sheringham Bower

The rhododendrons in my garden,
planted fifty-five years ago,
have stout trunks and massive
crowns, smothered with flowers
in shades of pink,
deep red, and pure white.
In addition to the blossoms,
I love their majestic stature
and handsome evergreen leaves
that provide a backdrop
for the flower beds.

What I see today stirs
the memory of Sheringham Bower
in England, a garden designed
by the great Capability Brown.
The name meant nothing
to me at the time.
I was seventeen, but I
have never forgotten the rolling
green meadows, Scotch pine, and
billows of rhododendron, as far
as the eye could see.

Change in the Neighborhood

We are old, my neighbors
and I, and have lived
in the same houses
for more than fifty years.
Our paperboy grew up
next door and recently retired
as a decorated general
in the Marine Corps.
The couple who live down
a long driveway—
out of sight but not
out of mind—have been
there for decades,
and so until this week
had my friend and attorney
in the white colonial
across the road from me.
But he is moving,
and our little community will
not be the same.

Shabby Comfort

I have a key
to my neighbor's old place,
where a cleaning lady is
vacuuming the pine floorboards.
There is nothing more forlorn
than an empty house—
walls denuded of artwork,
bookshelves bare of books.
Above the kitchen sink,
a water stain mars
the white ceiling.
While the leak was fixed
long ago, painting must have
seemed too disruptive,
so the years slipped by
in shabby comfort.

Sounds of the Sea

It has been unusually mild
this October, and today a
warm wind whips through
the trees with a hissing
sound, like the incoming tide
rushing up the ocean beaches
on Cape Cod. My family
went there in the fall.
The tourists had left, and
the water was still warm,
but Dad and I were
the only swimmers.
Otherwise the beaches were deserted.
I remember those days fondly—
the briny smell, the rhythm
of the waves going out
and coming in,
the cry of the gulls
flying low over the water,
and sandpipers running
along the firm, wet sand.
I miss the sea.

Precious Places

I know Echo Valley Road
the way my younger brother
and I knew our brook—
every inch, every pool,
every tussock of marsh grass.
When he was dying,
we would talk on the phone,
he from his coast,
I from mine, three thousand
miles away, and we would
walk together along the stream.
If ever my mind forgets,
my heart will always remember
these two precious places—the
road where I live and
the brook of my youth.

Full Circle

My mind is taken up
with thoughts of the ashes
in my attic.
A memorial service
for my older brother
took place five years ago,
but this final parting
has been easy to postpone.
Now his son and daughter
are coming east from Arizona
and California
to carry out his last
wish—to be buried
in the village
where my siblings
and I grew up.
Our parents are buried here,
soon to be joined
by their firstborn son—
apple of his mother's eye—
completing the circle
of another life.

A Good Place to Rest

Standing at the graveside
in two inches of snow,
the first of the season,
we bowed our heads
while the priest read
the prayer of Saint Francis
over my brother's ashes.
It was what he wanted,
to lie near his parents
in this old cemetery among
lichen-covered stones bearing dates
from the seventeen hundreds.
Whole families are buried here:
fathers, mothers, children,
and infants with angels
carved into their small headstones.
The setting is peaceful, overlooking
the Pomperaug River valley,
a good place
to spend eternity.

One More Set

It is cold and sunny
on the day my niece
and I revisit the cemetery
where her father is buried.
We close our eyes and
pray to the God
in whom, with fervent hearts,
we both want to believe.
At our feet, a stone
bears the names
of my parents, her grandparents.
She is here to arrange
for a similar stone
to mark her father's grave:
his name and the words
"One more set,"
as befits a jazz musician.

The Blue House

The town where I live
still boasts semi-rural roads,
like Hanover, which forks right
at the War Memorial.
A mile from town
on this road
is a blue house,
immaculately maintained
by a single woman.
I have always admired
her self-sufficiency: in the winter
she plows her own driveway,
and in the summer, launches
her boat on Lake Lillinonah.
But I have not seen
her lately and wonder
what has happened.
I will probably never know
but will think about her
whenever I pass by.

The Generations

I had not seen
the girl at my door
since the memorial service
for her grandmother, my friend
and neighbor of many years.
But I knew them all—
three generations of beautiful women
with skin as smooth
and fine as bone china.
I remember her mother's wedding
on a foggy December evening
in the 1960s.
My husband and I
caught a glimpse
of the bride, illuminated
in the low beam
of our headlights, as she
ran up the front steps
of her parents' house—
the white dress,
her white neck and arms,
radiant in the semi-darkness.
Today her daughter has come
for a visit—the same
exquisite pallor,
but with her own
high cheekbones and
a wide smile that makes
the heart sing.

A Well-Guarded Secret

I was so happy but
always frightened, knowing
that someday he would die.
For years, that knowledge
remained in the vault
of my heart, guarded
like a guilty secret.
He knew, but I think
he had more confidence
in me than I had
in myself, and he must
have been right,
because I am still alive
and there is no room
in my heart for anything
except love and gratitude.

New Purpose

Life had form and meaning
while my husband was alive.
But after his death,
every day had to be
reinvented and new purpose found.
That's why I sometimes sit
at the kitchen table
in his chair—the one
with arms—wondering
what to do next.
Today the dog and I
will meet a young friend
who teaches writing
to fifth graders.
He and I will walk
and talk about poetry
while Phoebe tugs
on her leash, occasionally
pausing to inspect a culvert.

Love Like No Other

I don't often feel lonely,
but there is always
an empty space where once
there was love,
exclusive, specific, and as deep
as the sea.
There is such a thing
as heartbreak, when overwhelming
sadness sweeps up the strand
and floods the hollow heart.
But the eternal ebb and
flow of living and dying
is the same for all,
and I am truly thankful
to have had this life
and love like no other.

The Memory of Love

I remember how love felt,
like an electric shock,
a convulsive joy coursing along
every nerve and sinew.
Throughout our life together,
there were these moments
when love would catch me
unaware, sending tremors
through my body and filling
my heart with thankfulness.
I remember them, but memory
is a poor substitute
for ecstasy.

Wherever You Are

I long for some manifestation
of your spirit.
In life, we were close.
For almost fifty years, you
filled my heart and mind.
Your death left emptiness,
a black hole that swallows
sight and sound.
I would give the world
to hear your voice again.
But then I couldn't bear
to let it go, because
I know what loneliness is.
It is not the desire
for company—I have friends,
loyal and kind.
But I will leave them
gladly to join you,
wherever you are.

Recurring Miracles

Third of January

A new year reveals itself
gradually, as the mist thins
and the temperature rises.
The sky is gray, but I
hear planes flying high
above the clouds, heading
for the New York airports.
Soon their passengers will be
fastening seat belts, turning off
electronic devices, and preparing
for the steep descent.
In the cockpit, pilots
call out numbers: five hundred,
four hundred, three hundred,
two hundred; approaching
minimum, one hundred, fifty, forty,
faster, faster, a sudden jolt
and wheels touch the tarmac.
On the ground in Connecticut,
noon has come and gone,
and rain is falling steadily
on this third day of January.

Waiting for a Sign

Under the pale, unfathomable sky,
we wait for a sign.
Snow is in the forecast,
and the garden seems
to hold itself in readiness.
Wildlife has already taken cover
under the dense juniper hedge,
and somewhere a crow calls.
Otherwise, only the distant rumble
of interstate traffic
disturbs the deep winter peace.

Winter Walk

We walked in the cold
as the sun was setting,
our pace brisk and businesslike,
with only brief pauses while
the dog considered her options:
leave a message
for the next dog now
or wait until later?
I made the decision with
a tug of her leash
and headed for the car,
still half a mile away.
At last! We made it.
And how good it felt
to finally be warm again!

Raptor

The white object bobbed up
and down, eye-catching
against the dark background
of leafless forest trees.
A bird? But what kind?
Binoculars separated the shape
into its component parts:
the snow-white head equipped
with a yellow bill, stout
and cruelly curved, tearing
bloody strips from the body
of a hapless squirrel.
When the meal was over,
a few heavy wingbeats
lifted the huge bird skyward,
heading for the Shepaug Dam,
winter gathering place
of bald eagles.

A Winter Morning in New England

New England winters are full
of contradictions—summer-blue skies
and frigid temperatures; the pristine
beauty of snow before
the town truck spews salt
and sand on the roads,
blackening banks on both sides.
But these will soon be
covered because
it is snowing again.
Sitting at the kitchen table,
I watch countless tiny flakes—
each different from the others
but uniform to me—
drifting down to the ground.
Inside, the floor is ten
degrees colder than my lap,
where the dog is asleep.

A World in Miniature

In my hand, I hold
a miniature world—a terrarium
inside a clear glass globe
four inches in diameter.
It was a Christmas gift
from a talented gardening friend,
whose nimble fingers unrolled
the tiny mat of moss
and planted partridge berry
and spotted wintergreen.
In the damp atmosphere
inside the globe, these woodland
plants are flourishing.
Instead of a flat carpet,
each minuscule moss plant
has become an upright thread,
which I examine
with a hand lens,
discovering fernlike side branches.
Now I have ordered books
about these fascinating plants
that once shared their world
with dinosaurs
many millions of years ago.

Early Flowering

Forcing a plant into premature
bloom sounds like cruel
and unusual punishment,
but early-flowering
witch hazel, forsythia,
and Japanese quince
do not seem to mind.
A few sprigs
clipped in January, brought indoors,
and placed in a vase
of water soon begin to
open their buds,
bringing the welcome
sight and scent of spring
into the house.

Unseasonable

On the last day of
the second month
in the year—new
such a short time ago—
spring peepers began singing
in the swamp, and killdeer
returned to Fairfield Hills.
Their anxious cries filled
the unseasonably mild air.
But that night, the temperature
plummeted to single digits.
Birds and tree frogs
fell silent, and daylight brought
little relief from the cold.
Weather in the Nutmeg State
prompted Mark Twain to say,
"If you don't like it,
wait a minute," and as
a native of Connecticut,
I have learned to do
just that, wait.

Smelling the Flowers

I have drifted through
the morning, just gazing
at the garden under a
gray February sky
and smelling the flowers.
The kitchen where I sit
is warm and fragrant
with the scent of hyacinths.
Their military bearing seems
too rigid in the garden.
But indoors, a few bulbs
in a pot can drive
winter away and fill a room
with a fragrance as light
and sweet as spring itself.

The Miracle of Spring

Spring is a recurring miracle
that ravishes the soul
with its tender beauty.
No blaze of color demands
attention nor sultry perfume
burdens the fresh, cool air.
Pale hues, the indescribable scent
of damp earth, and snowdrops,
modestly nodding their heads,
herald this most welcome
of all seasons.

Flowering Lawn

In my garden, lawn is
an open space covered
with ground-hugging plants
all about the same height.
It includes the heart-shaped leaves
of violets, jagged rosettes
of dandelions, clover, and mazus,
a little plant
with mauve blossoms.
While some grass has survived
from numerous fall sowings,
there is no irrigation system,
and rock ledge lies
close to the surface.
In the summer, there are
always brown spots.
But in the spring,
my lawn exhibits
an unruly charm, speckled
as it is with flowers.

Spent Bloom

The rushing green days
of spring accumulate
in carpets of spent bloom—
innumerable pink-tinted bells
beneath the enkianthus, a tree
of small stature but great charm.
I scoop up a handful
of blossoms to study
their red veins and edges.
Nearby, the rhododendron flowers
wane gracelessly.
I used to remove them,
but now these mighty shrubs
are fifteen feet tall, and
I simply avert my eyes
until the fresh new foliage
covers their temporary shame.

Here Today and Gone Tomorrow

Soon it will be hot,
but in the relative cool
of morning, rising sap
fills every stem, leaf, petal,
and blade of grass, and
gratitude fills my heart.
In fifty years of gardening,
I have never seen
so many daylilies
flowering together in colors
that beggar description.
But part of their allure
is the ephemeral nature
of their beauty.
Each perfect flower blooms
for one day only—
here today and gone tomorrow.

Glad Summer

This first day of summer
is the perfect summer's day—
warm but not hot; sunny
and filled with birdsong.
Ample spring rain has restored
the water table to normal,
and a few miles away,
the shallow Pomperaug River glides
smoothly over its rocky bed.
Here in my garden,
all the green things that
make up the lawn are
luxuriant, and at this moment,
in this day I will
surely rejoice and be glad.

Gratitude

Under a cloudy summer sky
I am drowning in beauty.
The daylilies are at their
peak in number and perfection,
hundreds of them.
Flattered by the soft morning
light, their warm colors
blend in unison,
like a chord of music.
The echo will stay
with me throughout the day
and into the evening,
when the flowers finally close.
For so much loveliness,
gratitude seems small recompense.

A Time to Every Purpose

Heavy-footed August has arrived
to spread heat and humidity
over the breathless landscape.
A house wren plows
through the thick, warm air
to feed a fledgling almost
as big as she is.
This is the month
of hanging on, letting go,
and enduring the vicissitudes
of a New England summer.
In the perennial borders, flowers
have dwindled down
to a handful, and
the annual pink poppies
have already gone to seed.
Living, dying, and carrying on—
it is the same
for man and beast.

August Ritual

In the garden, each season
has its rituals, and August
is the time to divide
daylilies, whose fleshy roots
give rise to arching foliage,
numerous flower-bearing scapes,
and weeks of
dawn-to-dusk bloom.
All they ask in return
is the division
of overgrown clumps.

Dig up the whole plant.
Drive two spading forks—
back to back—
into the tangle of roots.
Gently push the fork handles
apart, splitting the clump in two.
Replant one half and
give the other away.
Everybody loves daylilies
because no plant gives
more pleasure for less work.

Hot Days and Tropical Nights

The August days drag on
and on—hot, sunny, and
still, except for the buzzing
of houseflies and the high-pitched
whine of cicadas.
Overhead, clouds drift slowly
from west to east, as
shadows lengthen across the lawn.
Already, the days are becoming
measurably shorter.
In the flower beds,
Sedum 'Autumn Joy' is beginning
to turn pink, and
the Joe-Pye weed, dusky rose.
The terrace is a jungle
of tender perennials dominated by
treelike brugmansias,
whose trumpet-shaped flowers
hang limp during the day
but miraculously tilt upward
as light leaves the sky,
pouring forth their sultry perfume
into the warm summer night.

New Morning

Curled up on my lap,
the dog adds her weight
and warmth to the heat
of this late summer morning.
I should water the pots,
but the will to action
is weak and the sky,
overcast; there is no urgency.
To the delight of gardeners
here in the Northeast,
lawns are still green, and
perennials, flourishing.
This season owes us nothing!
Sitting here, the doors
wide open, I have watched
the thinning clouds.
Phoebe jumps off my knee;
I open the screen door,
and we both go out
to greet the day.

The Survivors

We are at the end
of a long, hot summer
with no rain for weeks.
The sugar maples are already
turning, but not
to the vivid fall colors
that traditionally attract
visitors to New England.
Instead, they have taken on
a hue like tarnished silver.
In the flower beds,
only the most adaptable perennials
are holding their own—daylilies,
ornamental grasses, and
reliable native plants
like asters and snakeroot,
the same ones that thrive
on Holcombe Hill
amid the acres of goldenrod
and tall bluestem grass.
These remnants of the prairie
have lessons to teach us.
The secret of their survival
is that they ask little
and stand up to competition.

Kindly Light

Rain, at last!
The relief is immeasurable.
From the overcast morning sky,
a gentle light infuses everything
with color: the lawn looks
green again, and the chartreuse
foliage of sweet potato vine,
spilling from pots
on the terrace, glows
as if lit from within.
Like a phototropic plant, I
incline toward brightness and light—
not the harsh flat light
of the midday sun but
the first and last
light of the day,
especially the latter.
When the time comes,
I will follow that light
as it fades slowly
from the hills.

The Rhythm of the Seasons

Why do I feel sad?
The summer has been beautiful,
with abundant rain, moderate temperatures,
and wave after wave
of color in the garden.
July belongs to the daylilies.
After that, only Joe-Pye weed
commands attention, followed by
Sedum 'Autumn Joy',
and finally the purple asters.
The melancholy I am feeling
is just the rhythm
of life and the seasons—
the great rush of spring
burgeoning into summer;
then, autumn harvest, and finally,
the deep stillness
of the long winter sleep.

Reprieve

Gusty winds from the north
tossed treetops in the wake
of Hurricane Matthew, and overnight
the temperature fell thirty degrees.
Inland, there were frost warnings.
But this time
we were spared, and today
the sun rose in golden
splendor, lifting spirits damped down
by thoughts of approaching winter.
There could still be weeks
of calm, dry days and
frost-free nights, but this rebirth
of summer is a gift
that can be snatched
away at a moment's notice.
Will it be tonight,
when the huge full moon
comes to rest
on the horizon?
Or later, when it's
on the wane?
We do not know and
are, in any case, powerless
before the forces of nature.

Sweet September

There is a sweet sadness
about the month of September,
a lingering regret for summer,
spent but not yet gone.
While no sound disturbs
the hush of early morning,
evenings throb with
the rasping of katydids,
as the earth breathes out
warmth absorbed during
the long, hot days
of July and August.
A new moon rises
into the black velvet night
strewn with stars.
When it comes
to the full and sets,
autumn will officially
have begun.

Flyway

On this quiet, summery morning
in mid-October,
the last sweet corn
has been picked, and
migratory birds are restless.
Soon they must begin
the long journey from
their northern breeding grounds to
winter quarters in the south,
where temperatures are mild,
and food, plentiful.
Connecticut is on their flyway.
This week, warblers of different kinds
have passed through, adding bright
yellow plumage to the golds
of the autumn landscape
and their trilling songs
to the sounds of the season.

Autumn Wind

A week ago, the forest
was tiger-striped in black
and gold—the trunks
of maples and tulip trees
dark against the tawny
understory foliage.
But last night torrential rain
and wind gusts
of sixty miles an hour
tore off leaves and limbs.

Along our road, power lines
were downed and telephone
service, interrupted.
Today is calm and mild,
as if nothing had happened.
But everywhere town trucks
and crews are busy
with chain saws.
Here, the woods are leafless
and ready now for winter.

Turning the Page

Rather than disturb the dog
sleeping in my lap,
I drink lukewarm tea
and watch the leafless trees
swaying back and forth
in a stiff northwest wind.
It has been blowing
nonstop for days now.
Yesterday the dog and I
cut short our walk.
Outward bound, the wind was
at our backs, but returning
we faced into a gale
that flipped Phoebe's ears
inside out and upright
and made me wish
I had worn a scarf.
It is that time before
the sun reaches
the Tropic of Capricorn
and reverses its course,
turning the page
from autumn to winter.

The Day Before Christmas

The lawn was still green
on the day before Christmas,
but during the night,
snow began to fall,
and by morning, the ground
was white and the trees
trimmed with ermine—
every branch and twig.
As the pale sun rose
above the hills, the landscape
was bathed in glorious light,
the kind that makes it
possible to suspend all disbelief.

Harvest of Years

Lessons from the Garden

The soft hiss of rain,
falling straight and steady,
is music to my ears,
and the moisture is balm
to the garden.
Gardens and gardeners are
entirely dependent upon nature.
That is the first lesson
gardening has taught me.
The second is patience—
being able to endure
ups and downs with equanimity.
I have been gardening
for more than fifty years
and still struggle with patience,
but I'm learning.

A Place for Art

There is a unique place
where young and not-so-young
adults with disabilities come together
to create works of art,
full of color and vitality.
Today sunlight floods the room
where they labor
at long tables.
One artist renders landscape in
tiny blocks of pure hue.
Another paints delicate flowers
that have never existed, except
in her imagination.
Art levels the playing field
because the source of inspiration
lies less in the head
than in the heart
and the enduring, indestructible spirit.

Cause and Effect

The source of a poem
is hard to pin down.
It can be a phrase,
God-given and surprising,
that acts like a magnet,
attracting other words
to its cause.
Or it can be
a strong feeling that pushes
its way into the mind
and cannot be denied.
But there has to be
an impetus, a booster rocket
to lift the weight
of the words
into the air,
where their sound and meaning
become accessible.

Hope

Will the words be there?
Or will that small voice
cease to whisper
in my ear about beauty
so intense and ephemeral
that it cuts through
to the soul?
Beauty is so like pain,
only the best poets
can tell the difference
and find the words.
I just hope and wait.

Continuum

They are too soon come
and gone—the days, months,
and years between childhood
and old age.
We try to capture time
by preserving memories, but only
in the here and now
does the hermit thrush sing
and the hawk's shadow pass
across the open lawn.
So look and listen deeply—
every single day.

Dreaming

Old skin tears
like tissue paper.
Casual contact with a corner
inflicts a wound that takes
weeks to heal
and leaves a scar.
It's no wonder the aged
do things carefully
and at a measured pace.
But sometimes we dream of
boldness and escape;
of riding horseback,
galloping and galloping
the length of the valley
where a river runs
behind the trees
on its way to freedom
and the open sea.

A Warning

I live the way baseball
players play the game—stealing
bases and sliding home by
the skin of my teeth!
I leave enough time
to get to appointments
if every light is green.
But a single stop sign,
and it is all over.
I have discovered that
young cops are especially stern
with old ladies who exceed
the speed limit.
On one occasion I explained
that I needed to walk
the dog before dark,
an argument that left
the officer shaking his head
as he returned to his vehicle,
having written me a warning.

Halcyon Days

Like New England weather,
life is unpredictable:
sunny one minute,
dark and stormy the next.
But in between, halcyon days
restore the balance.
According to legend,
Alcyone, daughter of the wind,
became a bird and built
a nest on the sea,
over which she cast
a magic spell of calm.
But after her fledglings
had left their birthplace, life
with its ups and downs
went on as before.

Perfect Peace

I spread my arms wide
and take a deep breath.
The air is always sweet
on this expansive hilltop.
A barn with beautiful proportions
and a gambrel roof overlooks
acres of pasture, where horses
graze in fields that slope
down to the valley floor.
Here corn stands
in endless rows,
and there is perfect peace.

Between Night and Day

We walked last night, caught
between night and day, sunset
behind us, moonrise before us.
While the departing sun flared
up in gold and purple,
the earth's satellite remained
as white as tissue paper,
a perfect circle of light,
floating upward from a blue-green
sea into the darkening sky.
It was cold now, but
we could not tear ourselves
away from the transforming
beauty of this dying day.

Families

In Germany, the time is
three o'clock in the afternoon
on the day when
an eagerly awaited grandchild
will be born or may
have already arrived.
Being a grandparent must be
the purest of pleasures!
And for first-time parents,
what joy and what apprehension!
No longer a couple,
from now on
they are a family.
And families are made
one day at a time.
Year by year, ever-changing relationships
are woven of love, laughter,
and tears; hope, belief, and
confidence in the future,
as all move forward together.

Thanksgiving

This morning every surface was
white with frost, but indoors
ovens have been heating up
kitchens since dawn.
It is Thanksgiving Day, and
family members are busy
peeling onions and chopping celery
for the stuffing, washing cranberries
and grating orange rind
for the relish.
Unlike Christmas, Thanksgiving
is about people, not presents.
Families of all kinds—those
related by birth, others
by choice and mutual affection—
gather together to express their
gratitude for each other and
all that we have.

Friendship

Friends are people you call
when the six-foot-tall tree
on the terrace blows over,
and you need another
pair of hands.
Or when you have done
something stupid, like
backing out of the garage
with the car door open.
When this happened to me,
I stood in the driveway
wringing my hands,
until a friend surveyed
the damage and said,
"So what? It's a car."

My walking friends are
in a class by themselves
because the pace is dictated
by a Jack Russell Terrier
with her own agenda.
We lurch forward when she
sees a squirrel and come
to an abrupt halt at
the foot of a tree.
Or we zigzag side to side
in pursuit of the illusive
scent of who knows what.
Friendship is about tolerance,
patience, and above all else,
just being there.

Plant by Plant

Gardens are full of stories.
The sea of pink poppies
in the cutting garden came
from a charming old gentleman
who gardened near Pittsburgh,
Pennsylvania, and was known
to younger gardeners as Uncle.
Farther north and west, the
Society of the Divine Word
was home to Brother Charles Reckamp,
famous for breeding daylilies with
ruffled edges and subtle colors.
His flowers are among
the loveliest in my garden.
And the lamb's ears edging
my long border were one
of many gifts from
my first gardening mentor.
This is how gardens
are made—plant by plant,
from one gardener to another.

Exquisite Geometry

How can we not believe
in a higher authority than
the ego that basks only
in its own reflection?
While egoism is busy looking
inward and seeing
nothing but self,
the tumultuous world of nature
abounds in other creatures
and their works.
Consider the exquisite geometry
of the chambered nautilus,
a seashell built hundreds
of millions of years ago
by mollusks, shapeless, soft-bodied
animals that remain, nevertheless,
among the oldest and most
successful of all living things.

On a Winter Afternoon

Yesterday I made a fire
in the sitting room fireplace
to banish the cold and wet
of a midwinter afternoon.
Gas fires are realistic and
convenient, but a wood fire
is so much more companionable
with its soft breathing sounds
and mesmerizing tongues of flame.
I had intended to read
but instead drank tea and
passed the time watching
the logs burn slowly,
until they collapsed and turned
first to embers
and finally to ashes.

Ordinary Days

Don't cast this day aside,
however ordinary it may seem.
When those ahead are fewer
than those behind,
each one counts, and
small things make a day—
a grilled cheese sandwich,
warm, gooey, and golden;
the casual compliment
from a stranger or
phone call from a friend.
What day is not improved
by a dog's ecstatic welcome
and warm companionship at night?
Mark every cloudless sky and
setting sun, because
we never know when
it will be the last.

Being Alive

In order to live fully,
we must not be afraid
of death because we die
a little every day, spending
our time and energies on
those we love and that
which pleases them and us.
That is life.
In youth, we demand answers
about its meaning.
In old age, we know
that being alive
means everything.

The Divine Word

God speaks in a voice
so soft that only
the attentive ear can
distinguish its sweet sound
from the birds calling and
the wind in the trees.
Shut your eyes and listen.
From behind the screen
of your closed lids,
it is easier to hear.
Now open the shutters,
and you will see beauty
in every blade of grass.

The Very Young

The world has turned again,
and precipitous spring is rushing
toward us, beautiful and bountiful.
Babies born last fall are
already learning to turn over.
Urged on by proud parents,
they grunt with effort and
gurgle happily when they succeed.
Before long, these babies
will be crawling and reaching
for a hand to grasp
in order to pull themselves
upright, swaying on unsteady legs
but triumphant.
Life flashes by so quickly
for the very young, and
for the very old.

My Treasures

My kitchen table is littered
with paperwork—
bills, paid and unpaid;
a bright pink notice
to residents of my town
from the fire marshall.
This seems to be
good news, something to do
with my homeowner's insurance.
Home owning is a job.
This month, I must pay
for my safe deposit box,
empty except for the deed
to this house.
I have no other valuables,
no jewelry—I'm too careless.

My treasures are pieces
of well-used antique furniture:
the nice Queen Anne table
from Martin's Aunt Edith
that is missing a foot;
an oak corner cupboard
from the front hall
of my parents' house, and
the little tavern table that
my mother bought in England
for my father, its rails
worn smooth by centuries
of plowmen's boots.
While these pieces have little
monetary value, their worth
to me is inestimable.

A Deadly Dance

In the skies over Britain
during the Second World War,
sleek Spitfires rose to meet
Messerschmitts escorting
German bombers on their way
to London, Coventry, and Norwich.
While the heavy aircraft lumbered
toward their targets, the swift,
well-armed fighter planes engaged
in a deadly dance—attacking
at such close quarters, pilots
could read each other's lips.
We know the outcome now
of the bombings and dogfights,
but we have never learned
how to keep them
from coming to pass.

The Things We Remember

Yesterday was the fifteenth anniversary
of the World Trade Center
attack that changed America and
every American then living or
born since, our complacency shattered
once and for all.
A shaken neighbor called that
day from the hardware store.
All he said was,
"Turn on the television."

We watched in disbelief
as the horror unfolded—
the low-flying aircraft crashing
into the south tower and
exploding in a fireball.
In seconds, flames and clouds
of black smoke obliterated the
upper floors, while sirens
screamed in streets below
as the mighty building shuddered,
began to crumble, and collapsed
while we looked on
in helpless anguish.

On that day, ordinary people
became heros, putting the safety
of others before their own—
the executive who led his
staff in the dark down
endless flights of stairs;
another who wouldn't leave
without his secretary;
and the firefighters who
rushed into danger because
their job was saving lives.
These things are what
we remember.

The God of Gates and Doorways

This is the last day
of the month that Romans
named for Janus, their two-faced
god of gates and doorways,
who looks simultaneously backward
at the past and forward
into the future.
What would he see today?
Behind us, a period
of relative calm; ahead, uncertainty
and conflict about who we are.
Will we slam shut gates
once flung wide to those
escaping persecution and famine?
Will we regard every stranger
with hostility and suspicion?
The answer seems to be
an uncharacteristic yes.
Please, Janus, look ahead
and see a different vision
of a wiser, kinder America.

Battleground

God breathes life
into our bodies but leaves
to our own devices
the soul, the part
of us that thinks,
feels, and desires.
In our incompetent hands,
we arrive at old age
with souls battered by time
and the lifelong struggle
between the best in us
and the worst—battling
it out until the end,
when it will matter less
what we thought than
what we did.

The Enemy

In old age, the enemy
is not death but fear—
the stealthy, creeping menace that
seizes optimism by the throat
and squeezes the pleasure
out of every joyful occasion.
Be happy if you can
and live in the moment,
knowing that all will be
well in the end.

Acknowledgments

As an editor, Lorraine Anderson is every writer's dream, someone with the power of seeing into the heart of things. She always gets the point and also knows the rules. For her patience, understanding, and professionalism, I am deeply grateful.

Artist and graphic designer Barbara Cottingham has again put her many gifts at my disposal. Her perceptive reading of the poems made a substantial contribution to the design of the book as a whole. She has made it beautiful to look at and a joy to peruse.

Kimberly Day Proctor, fine artist, photographer, and good friend, took the cover photo. To me, it seems the perfect introduction to this book of poems about the seasons of life: the aged gardener and the fifty-six-year-old wheelbarrow with giant rhododendrons in the background, planted when they were the size of bushel baskets.

I have loved working with this trio of extremely talented women. They lift my spirits with their encouragement and enthusiasm and sustain my belief in the poetry.

Animal photographer, friend, and fellow dog enthusiast Hank Meirowitz took the back cover photo.

Other kind friends have lent an ear and provided moral support: Marilyn Rennegal and Barbara Bixby; my sisters-in-law, Nancy Webber and Marianna Webber; my niece, Jeni Webber, a gifted landscape architect who loves gardens as much as I do; our mutual friend, the photographer, writer, and editor Lee Anne White.

I am also grateful to Anne and John Harrigan, who have helped me in a thousand ways, and to Kathy Kling, whose hard work in my garden and sense of humor have kept me going and the garden in good order. Her passion for gardening is a delight and an inspiration.

*S*ydney Eddison lives with her Jack Russell Terrier, Phoebe, in a yellow farmhouse surrounded by a 2½-acre garden of her own creation in Newtown, Connecticut. Her articles have appeared in publications such as *Fine Gardening* and *Horticulture,* and she is the award-winning author of seven books on gardening, including *Gardening for a Lifetime, A Passion for Daylilies,* and *A Patchwork Garden.* This is her third book of poetry.

Made in the USA
Columbia, SC
30 December 2020

28756440R00064